About the Author

Growing up in the inner-city housing projects, he knew the odds were stacked against him. Dropping out of high school didn't make things any easier. But instead of succumbing to his circumstances, he was determined to change his life. Through sheer grit and determination, he taught himself the principles of business acquisition and wealth-building. Using the very steps outlined in The Business Acquisition Manifesto, he acquired businesses in HVAC services, electrical, plumbing, fine dining restaurants, and landscaping.

Through smart business acquisitions, he built a portfolio with over $2.75 million in assets under management (AUM) and leveraged those earnings to expand into real estate. Now, with over $1.95 million invested in real estate across more than 75 doors, he has created a legacy that defies the odds and redefines the possibilities for those who come from humble beginnings. Today, his story is a testament to the power of strategic planning, perseverance, and business ownership.

His journey is proof that anyone, no matter their background, can achieve financial freedom and build generational wealth with the right blueprint.

Prepare Your Personal Credit

Step 1: Prepare Your Personal Credit

Your personal credit score is the foundation for securing business funding and the SBA 7(a) loan needed for a business acquisition. Lenders, including banks and the SBA, will assess your creditworthiness to ensure you are a responsible borrower. A strong credit profile not only helps you qualify for favorable loan terms but also influences the amount of business credit and loans you can access.

Why Your Personal Credit Matters
Lenders view your personal credit score as an indicator of your financial habits and reliability. For a business acquisition, especially when dealing with loans like the SBA 7(a), personal credit is scrutinized even if the business is being purchased under a separate legal entity like an LLC. A poor credit score can result in higher interest rates, reduced loan amounts, or outright disqualification for business funding.

Credit Score Requirements
While each lender has specific guidelines, here are general benchmarks:
- 680 or Higher: This is typically the minimum credit score you should aim for to qualify for most business acquisition loans. Some lenders may work with lower scores, but a score of 680 or higher will give you access to better loan terms and funding opportunities.
- 720+: A score above 720 opens doors to more competitive interest rates, lower down payments, and a wider range of loan products.

Steps to Improve and Maintain Your Credit Score

1. Check Your Credit Report
   Begin by pulling your credit reports from all three major credit bureaus—Experian, Equifax, and TransUnion. Under the Fair

Credit Reporting Act, you are entitled to one free credit report from each bureau annually via [AnnualCreditReport.com](https://www.annualcreditreport.com). Review your report for errors or inaccuracies, such as incorrect late payments, accounts that don't belong to you, or outdated information.

If you find errors, file disputes with the respective credit bureaus to have these corrected. Errors can drag down your score unnecessarily, so it's crucial to clear them up before starting the business acquisition process.

2. Pay Down Credit Card Balances

Your credit utilization ratio—how much of your available credit you're using—makes up 30% of your credit score. Aim to keep your credit utilization below 30%, but ideally, you should target 10% or less. For example, if your total credit limit across all cards is $50,000, try to maintain balances below $15,000.

If you have high balances, work to reduce them before seeking funding. You can pay off debt faster by using strategies such as:
- The Snowball Method: Focus on paying off your smallest debt first, then move to the next smallest, while making minimum payments on the rest.
- The Avalanche Method: Focus on paying off debt with the highest interest rate first, then move to the next highest.

3. Avoid Late Payments

Payment history is the most critical factor in determining your credit score, accounting for 35% of your total score. Missed payments stay on your credit report for up to seven years, so it's essential to make all credit card, loan, and bill payments on time. Set up automatic payments or calendar reminders to ensure you never miss a due date.

If you've had late payments in the past, time is your best ally. Focus on maintaining a clean payment history going forward, as recent positive activity will gradually outweigh older late payments.

4. Diversify Your Credit Mix

Lenders prefer to see that you can responsibly manage different types of credit, including revolving accounts (credit cards) and installment accounts (auto loans, personal loans, or mortgages). If your credit profile only includes one type of account, consider adding diversity by taking out a small installment loan or applying for a new credit card (if your utilization is low).

However, don't open too many accounts at once, as this could lower your average account age and lead to a temporary drop in your score. Ideally, space out new credit inquiries and allow accounts to age naturally.

5. Limit Hard Inquiries

Each time you apply for credit, a hard inquiry is added to your credit report. Multiple hard inquiries within a short period can negatively impact your score. Try to limit new credit applications, especially in the months leading up to your business acquisition, to avoid a dip in your score.

If you're rate-shopping for a loan, such as a mortgage or car loan, multiple inquiries within a short window (typically 14-45 days) are usually treated as a single inquiry by FICO, minimizing the impact on your score.

6. Build a Positive Credit History with Secured Credit Cards

If your credit is currently weak or you're rebuilding it after financial struggles, consider using secured credit cards. These cards require a deposit and offer a way to build a positive credit history. The deposit acts as collateral, so they are easier to qualify for even with lower credit scores.

By making small purchases and paying them off in full each month, you can steadily improve your credit score without accumulating high-interest debt.

Debt-to-Income Ratio (DTI)

While your credit score is critical, lenders will also consider your debt-to-income ratio when reviewing your application for business loans. Your DTI compares the total amount of your monthly debt payments to your gross monthly income. Most lenders prefer a DTI below 43%, though lower is always better.

For example, if your total monthly debt payments (including rent or mortgage, car payments, and any loans) total $3,000 and your gross monthly income is $8,000, your DTI is 37.5%. Reducing your DTI before applying for loans can increase your chances of approval and lower your interest rates.

Boosting Your Credit Score Quickly

If you need to raise your score within a short period (e.g., 3 to 6 months), here are some rapid strategies:

1. **Become an Authorized User:** If a family member or friend has a credit card with a long history of on-time payments and a low balance, you can ask to become an authorized user on their account. Their positive history will reflect on your credit report, boosting your score.

2. **Request a Credit Limit Increase:** Increasing your credit limit can immediately lower your utilization ratio, provided you don't increase your spending. Many banks allow you to request credit limit increases online or via phone without a hard inquiry.

3. **Pay Bills Twice a Month:** If your credit card reports balances to the credit bureaus before you've made your payment, paying your bill twice a month can reduce the balance reflected in your credit report, lowering your utilization rate.

4. Use Credit Builder Loans: Credit builder loans are designed to help individuals build credit. The loan amount is typically held in a secured account, and you make payments over time. Once the loan is fully paid, the funds are released to you, and the positive payment history is reported to the credit bureaus.

Maintaining Strong Credit for the Long-Term

Even after you've secured the business funding and SBA loan, maintaining strong personal credit is essential for future business endeavors. Here's how you can ensure your credit stays healthy:

- Monitor Your Credit: Regularly review your credit reports to stay informed of any changes, errors, or potential identity theft. Many credit card issuers provide free credit score monitoring as a perk.
- Keep Accounts Open: Closing old credit accounts can hurt your score by reducing your available credit and lowering the average age of your accounts. Keep older, low-interest accounts open, even if you don't use them frequently.
- Continue Building Credit History: Use your credit cards for small, manageable purchases and pay them off in full each month to keep your credit active and growing.

By focusing on improving and maintaining your personal credit score, you'll position yourself to secure the business funding and loans you need for a successful acquisition.

Establish Your LLC

Step 2: Establish Your LLC

Setting up a Limited Liability Company (LLC) is a crucial step in the business acquisition process. An LLC is a flexible business structure that provides legal protection by separating your personal assets from your business liabilities. It also allows you to streamline taxation and create a formal structure for your business operations. For those planning to acquire an existing business, forming an LLC early on ensures you can transact under a legal entity, making it easier to secure loans, handle tax matters, and limit your personal liability.

Why Forming an LLC is Important for Business Acquisition

1. Liability Protection: One of the most significant advantages of forming an LLC is that it shields your personal assets (like your home, car, or savings) from the debts and liabilities of the business. In the case of lawsuits or debts incurred by the business, creditors can only go after the LLC's assets, not your personal ones.

2. Tax Flexibility: LLCs offer flexibility in taxation. You can choose to be taxed as a sole proprietorship, partnership, S corporation, or C corporation, depending on what's most advantageous for your business and financial situation. Many LLC owners opt for pass-through taxation, where profits are taxed on the owner's personal income tax return, avoiding corporate taxes.

3. Professionalism and Credibility: Having an LLC lends credibility to your business, which can be critical when dealing with lenders, vendors, and potential clients. It shows that you're serious and professional, and it allows you to open business bank accounts and secure business credit more easily.

4. Ease of Management: Unlike corporations, LLCs have fewer formalities to adhere to. There's no need for a board of directors,

annual meetings, or strict record-keeping requirements, which makes them ideal for small business owners.

Steps to Form Your LLC

1. Choose a Business Name

The first step in forming your LLC is choosing a business name. Your name should reflect the nature of your business while being unique and distinguishable from other businesses in your state.

- Naming Rules: Each state has its own guidelines for LLC names. In general, your business name must include "LLC" or "Limited Liability Company" and cannot contain words restricted by your state (e.g., "bank" or "insurance").
- Check Availability: Use your state's business name database to ensure the name you want is available. You can usually find this tool on your Secretary of State's website.
- Domain Name: It's also wise to check if the corresponding domain name is available for your business's website. Securing a matching domain will help establish your business's online presence.

2. File Articles of Organization

To legally form your LLC, you must file a document called the "Articles of Organization" (sometimes called a Certificate of Formation) with the Secretary of State's office or the relevant state agency. This document typically requires the following information:
- Business Name: The official name of your LLC.
- Business Address: The primary location of your business.
- Registered Agent: The individual or company designated to receive legal documents on behalf of the LLC. The registered agent must have a physical address in the state where you are forming the LLC.

- Ownership and Management Structure: Indicate whether your LLC will be managed by its members (owners) or by appointed managers.

3. Create an Operating Agreement

While not required in all states, it's highly recommended that LLCs create an Operating Agreement. This internal document outlines how the LLC will be run, including:
- Ownership Structure: Define the ownership percentages of each member if your LLC has multiple owners.
- Roles and Responsibilities: Clarify each owner's role in the business and decision-making processes.
- Profit Distribution: Outline how profits and losses will be shared among members.
- Dispute Resolution: Set rules for resolving disputes among owners, as well as the process for adding or removing members.

Having an Operating Agreement not only helps avoid future conflicts but also reinforces the limited liability status of your LLC by demonstrating that the business is a separate entity from its owners.

4. Obtain an Employer Identification Number (EIN)

Once your LLC is formed, you'll need to apply for an Employer Identification Number (EIN) with the IRS. This nine-digit number acts as your business's tax identification number, similar to a Social Security number but for your LLC. It's used for several essential tasks, including:
- Filing taxes
- Hiring employees
- Opening a business bank account
- Applying for business credit or loans

Applying for an EIN is free and can be done easily through the IRS website or by mail.

5. Open a Business Bank Account

One of the most critical steps in maintaining the legal and financial separation between your personal and business assets is opening a dedicated business bank account. This helps you track business income and expenses and prevents the commingling of funds, which could jeopardize your liability protection. You'll need your LLC formation documents and EIN to open the account.

A business bank account allows you to:
- Deposit business revenue
- Pay business expenses: Using a business debit card or writing checks in the name of the LLC ensures you maintain clear financial records.
- Access business credit and loans: When applying for business funding or loans, a business bank account is a key requirement.

6. Apply for Necessary Business Licenses and Permits

Depending on the nature of the business you plan to acquire and the state or local jurisdiction, you may need certain licenses or permits to operate legally. This could include:
- General business licenses
- Industry-specific licenses (e.g., restaurants, healthcare providers, contractors)
- Zoning permits

You can check with your state's business licensing office or local government agencies to ensure you have all the necessary permits in place.

7. File for Foreign LLC Status (if applicable)

If you plan to acquire a business in a state different from where you formed your LLC, you may need to file for "foreign LLC" status in the state where you'll operate. This essentially registers your

LLC to do business in another state. The process involves filing paperwork with the new state's government and paying any associated fees.

Key Considerations When Forming Your LLC

1. Single-Member vs. Multi-Member LLC:
   - A single-member LLC is simpler to set up, but the owner is taxed as a sole proprietor, meaning all profits and losses are reported on your personal tax return.
   - A multi-member LLC has multiple owners and is usually taxed as a partnership, with profits and losses passed through to the individual owners, who report them on their personal tax returns. For business acquisitions, you may prefer a multi-member LLC, especially if you plan to bring on partners or investors.

2. Series LLCs:
   Some states offer the option of forming a Series LLC, which allows you to segregate assets and liabilities among separate series (or divisions) under a single LLC. This can be particularly useful if you plan to acquire multiple businesses, as each series operates independently and shields the assets of other series from liabilities.

3. Taxation Options:
   As an LLC owner, you can choose how your business is taxed:
   - Sole Proprietorship/Partnership: Pass-through taxation means that profits are taxed at the individual level, avoiding double taxation.
   - S Corporation: You can elect to have your LLC taxed as an S corporation, which allows owners to pay themselves a salary and reduce self-employment taxes on the remaining profits.
   - C Corporation: If you anticipate significant profits and plan to reinvest in the business, you may opt for C corporation taxation, which allows for more flexible tax deductions.

Maintaining Your LLC

Once your LLC is established, there are a few ongoing responsibilities to keep in mind:

1. Annual Reports: Many states require LLCs to file an annual report or statement of information. This keeps the state updated on your LLC's current address, ownership, and registered agent. Be sure to mark your calendar, as missing this deadline can result in penalties or suspension of your LLC.

2. Tax Filings: Whether you choose pass-through taxation or elect a corporate tax status, make sure to file the appropriate tax forms and pay any taxes owed to the IRS and your state.

3. Keep Business and Personal Finances Separate: Maintaining the distinction between personal and business finances is crucial. Always pay yourself through the LLC, and avoid using business funds for personal expenses, as this can jeopardize the limited liability protection your LLC provides.

Secure 0% Interest Business Funding for 12+ Months

Step 3: Secure 0% Interest Business Funding for 12+ Months

One of the most strategic ways to fund a business acquisition is by securing 0% interest business funding. This type of funding allows you to borrow money without paying interest for an initial period—typically 12 months or more—giving you the flexibility to use the funds for a down payment or to cover operational expenses while avoiding high-interest charges. This step explains how to identify the right funding options, secure 0% interest business lines or credit cards, and utilize the funds effectively to prepare for your business acquisition.

Why 0% Interest Business Funding is Valuable

Securing business funding at 0% interest can be a game-changer, especially for business acquisitions, where you may need to raise capital for a down payment, closing costs, or initial operating expenses. Here's why it's beneficial:

1. No Interest Costs During the Introductory Period: With 0% interest, every dollar you borrow goes directly toward your acquisition or business expenses, without being eaten up by high interest rates. This gives you a longer runway to generate returns from your business before worrying about loan payments or interest charges.

2. Build Business Credit: Properly using a 0% interest credit card or business line of credit can help you build a strong business credit profile. This will be advantageous in the future when you need to secure additional funding for expansion or other business ventures.

3. Flexible Repayment: During the 0% interest period, you can make lower minimum payments, giving you the flexibility to use the capital to grow the business, increase cash flow, and manage operations.

4. Seasoning Funds for a Down Payment: Once you've secured the 0% interest funding, you can place it in your personal checking or business account to "season" the funds. This seasoning period (typically 60 to 90 days) makes it easier to demonstrate to lenders that you have the liquid assets required for a down payment when applying for a larger loan, such as an SBA 7(a) loan.

Step-by-Step Guide to Securing 0% Interest Business Funding

1. Evaluate Your Creditworthiness

Before applying for 0% interest business credit cards or lines of credit, it's essential to evaluate your personal and business credit profiles. Lenders use both to determine whether you qualify for business credit and what terms they can offer.

- Personal Credit Score: Ideally, you want your personal credit score to be 680 or higher. Higher scores will qualify you for better terms and larger credit limits.
- Business Credit Score: If you've already started an LLC or have an existing business, check your business credit score (through Dun & Bradstreet or similar services). A strong business credit profile will increase your chances of qualifying for higher credit limits.

If your personal or business credit score is not where it needs to be, revisit Step 1 of this guide to work on improving it before moving forward with funding applications.

2. Research Lenders and Credit Card Issuers

Not all credit cards or lenders offer 0% interest business funding. To find the best options, focus on credit cards or business lines of credit that provide an introductory 0% APR for at least 12 months. Here are several lenders and credit card issuers that are known for offering favorable 0% interest terms:

1. Chase Ink Business Cash® Credit Card:

- Introductory Rate: 0% APR for the first 12 months on purchases.
- Perks: Earn cash back on common business purchases like office supplies and internet services.
- Benefits: No annual fee and cash back opportunities make this a great card for general business use.

2. Bank of America Business Advantage Cash Rewards Mastercard®:
- Introductory Rate: 0% APR for the first 9 to 12 months on purchases.
- Perks: Cashback rewards on gas, office supplies, and dining.
- Benefits: Flexibility in choosing where to earn the highest cashback rate each month, and no annual fee.

3. American Express Blue Business Cash™ Card:
- Introductory Rate: 0% APR for the first 12 months on purchases.
- Perks: Earn 2% cash back on the first $50,000 in purchases each year, with no annual fee.
- Benefits: Ideal for businesses with regular purchases, and a long introductory period for 0% APR.

4. Wells Fargo Business Platinum Credit Card:
- Introductory Rate: 0% APR for 9-12 months on purchases.
- Perks: Earn points or cashback on everyday business expenses.
- Benefits: A solid option for businesses looking for flexible repayment and rewards without an annual fee.

5. Navy Federal Credit Union Business Credit Card (For eligible members):
- Introductory Rate: 0% APR on purchases for up to 12 months.
- Perks: No annual fee and flexible terms for veterans and military personnel.
- Benefits: Ideal for those who are eligible for membership and want to leverage credit union resources.

6. U.S. Bank Business Platinum Card:
   - Introductory Rate: 0% APR on purchases and balance transfers for the first 15 months.
   - Perks: No annual fee and low balance transfer fees.
   - Benefits: This card offers one of the longest 0% interest periods, which is ideal if you need extended time to repay the balance.

3. Apply for Multiple Credit Options (Strategically)
To maximize your funding potential, consider applying for multiple 0% interest business credit cards or lines of credit. This strategy can provide you with more capital and diversify your funding sources, reducing the risk of hitting credit limits early on.

- Stagger Applications: Apply for 1-2 credit cards at a time to avoid multiple hard inquiries hitting your credit report simultaneously, which can lower your score.
- Focus on Cards with High Credit Limits: Depending on your credit score and financial history, some cards may offer higher credit limits than others. Aim for cards that offer $10,000 or more in available credit.

4. Use Credit Lines Wisely
Once you've secured the 0% interest business funding, it's critical to manage it properly to avoid overspending or harming your credit profile. Here are a few tips:

1. Do Not Max Out the Credit: While it may be tempting to use the full credit limit, keeping your credit utilization low (below 30% of your total available credit) will help protect your personal and business credit scores. For example, if you receive $50,000 in credit limits, avoid using more than $15,000 at a time unless absolutely necessary.

2. Focus on Key Business Expenses: Use the 0% interest funding primarily for acquisition-related expenses such as:

- Down payments for the business acquisition
- Closing costs
- Initial operational expenses (inventory, staffing, marketing)
- Equipment upgrades or repairs

3. Track Spending: Keep careful records of all business-related expenses charged to the credit lines. This will help when reconciling your finances and filing taxes.

5. Place the Funds in a Checking Account for Seasoning
Once you've secured the funding, transfer it to a personal checking account or your business bank account to season the funds. The seasoning period refers to the amount of time money has been sitting in your account before lenders will recognize it as valid proof of funds. Most lenders prefer that funds used for a down payment have been in an account for at least 60-90 days.

By having this capital readily available, you demonstrate liquidity to the SBA or other lenders, which increases your credibility and loan approval chances for your business acquisition.

- Personal Checking Account: Place the funds here if you plan to use personal finances for the down payment.
- Business Checking Account: If the funds are tied to your LLC, deposit them in your business account for use in the acquisition process.

6. Create a Repayment Plan
Even though you won't have to pay interest for 12 or more months, it's important to have a solid plan for repaying the debt before the 0% interest period expires. After the introductory period, interest rates can skyrocket to 15% or higher, depending on the card issuer or lender.

- Monthly Payments: Calculate what you need to pay each month to fully repay the debt within the interest-free period. For example, if you borrowed $30,000 with a 12-month 0% interest period, you would need to pay approximately $2,500 per month to clear the balance before interest starts accruing.

- Balance Transfers: If you're unable to repay the full amount before the 0% period ends, consider transferring the remaining balance to another 0% interest credit card to extend your interest-free period.

Avoiding Pitfalls When Using 0% Interest Funding

1. Avoid Cash Advances: Many 0% interest credit cards do not extend the 0% APR to cash advances, and cash advances often carry high fees and immediate interest charges. Avoid using your credit cards for cash advances unless absolutely necessary.

2. Beware of Penalties: Missing a payment or exceeding your credit limit can result in losing the 0% APR offer. Be diligent in tracking your payments and staying within your credit limits to avoid these penalties.

3. Do Not Treat It as Free Money: While 0% interest funding is an excellent tool for business acquisitions, it's still debt. Make sure you have a repayment plan and ensure you can manage the debt responsibly. Treat it as a business investment that you need to pay back strategically within the interest-free period to avoid accumulating unnecessary financial burdens.

Step-by-Step Example: Using 0% Interest Funding for a Business Acquisition

Let's go through a real-world example to demonstrate how you could use 0% interest funding in a business acquisition:

1. Assess Your Financial Needs: You've identified a business you want to acquire, priced at $750,000. You need to make a down payment of 10%, or $75,000, and cover some closing costs (e.g., legal fees, appraisal, etc.), which amount to $10,000. Additionally,

you'll need $15,000 for operational expenses in the first few months after taking over the business. In total, you need $100,000 in funding.

2. Apply for Multiple Credit Options: After evaluating your personal and business credit scores, you apply for three different 0% interest business credit cards:
   - Chase Ink Business Cash®: Approved for a $30,000 credit line with 0% APR for 12 months.
   - Bank of America Business Advantage Cash Rewards Mastercard®: Approved for a $25,000 credit line with 0% APR for 9 months.
   - American Express Blue Business Cash™ Card: Approved for a $50,000 credit line with 0% APR for 12 months.

You now have $105,000 in available credit at 0% interest for at least 9 to 12 months, which is more than enough to cover your $100,000 in acquisition-related expenses.

3. Utilize the Funds Strategically:
   - Down Payment: Transfer $75,000 from your 0% interest credit cards into your personal or business bank account to season the funds for the down payment. These funds will sit in the account for 60-90 days, showing lenders that you have liquidity.
   - Closing Costs: Use $10,000 of your 0% interest funds to cover legal fees, appraisals, and other closing costs.
   - Operational Expenses: The remaining $15,000 can be used for inventory purchases, payroll, marketing, or any other business needs as you take over the new company.

4. Monitor the Seasoning Period: Allow the funds to sit in your account for the necessary seasoning period before applying for your SBA 7(a) loan. Lenders will require proof that these funds have been available for at least 60-90 days before they are used as a down payment.

5. **Apply for an SBA 7(a) Loan**: After the seasoning period, apply for the SBA 7(a) loan to cover the remaining $675,000 of the acquisition cost. With your down payment and credit history, you have a strong chance of getting approved for the loan.

6. **Repayment Plan**:
   - Set a repayment schedule to ensure that the $100,000 borrowed through the 0% interest business credit lines is repaid before the 0% APR period ends. For example, if you plan to repay the full $100,000 within 12 months, you'll need to allocate roughly $8,333 per month toward paying down the credit card debt. This can be done through profits generated by the newly acquired business or by refinancing through a longer-term loan if necessary.

7. **Balance Transfers (Optional)**: If you're unable to pay off the full balance before the 0% interest period ends, consider transferring the remaining balance to a new 0% interest credit card to extend your interest-free period. Just be aware that balance transfers often come with fees, so make sure the math works in your favor.

How to Prepare for the Post-0% Interest Period

Even with the best intentions and planning, there's always the possibility that you won't be able to repay the full balance before the 0% interest period ends. If this happens, here's how to prepare:

1. **Reassess Cash Flow**: Take a closer look at your business's cash flow. Are there any areas where you can increase revenue or cut costs? Can you make larger payments to reduce the debt more quickly?

2. **Consider Refinancing Options**: If the interest rates on your business credit cards are set to increase significantly after the 0% period, consider refinancing the remaining balance with a lower-

interest business loan. Look for lenders who offer small business loans or lines of credit with favorable terms.

3. Negotiate Payment Terms: Some credit card issuers are willing to negotiate lower interest rates or extended repayment terms, especially if you've been a good customer and made your payments on time.

4. Explore SBA Loans or Other Financing Options: The SBA offers a variety of loan programs that might help you refinance business credit card debt. Depending on your business's financial health, you may also qualify for term loans or working capital loans through traditional banks or alternative lenders.

Season Funds for the Down Payment

Step 4: Season Funds for the Down Payment

Once you've secured 0% interest business funding, the next step is to season the funds for your down payment on the business acquisition. "Seasoning" refers to the process of leaving money in a bank account for a specified period (usually 60 to 90 days) before using it as part of a larger transaction, such as a business acquisition. Lenders, including those offering SBA loans, require proof that the down payment funds have been in your possession for an adequate period to ensure you're not using borrowed or unstable funds that could jeopardize the transaction.

Why Seasoning is Important

1. Lender Confidence: Lenders prefer seasoned funds because it shows that you have stable, readily available liquid assets. This reduces their risk, as they are assured you aren't relying on last-minute loans or risky capital sources to meet your financial obligations.

2. Compliance with SBA Loan Requirements: The SBA 7(a) loan program, as well as many conventional business loans, require that down payment funds are seasoned for at least 60 to 90 days. This helps ensure that the borrower is financially stable and has demonstrated the ability to save and manage their finances.

3. Proof of Financial Stability: Showing that you've held onto a significant sum of money in your account for several months demonstrates financial discipline, which increases your chances of securing the loan. It also reassures lenders that you're not at risk of defaulting on your loan obligations.

Step-by-Step Guide to Seasoning Funds

1. Transfer the 0% Interest Funds into a Checking Account

After securing 0% interest business funding through credit cards or lines of credit (outlined in Step 3), the first thing you need to do is transfer these funds into a bank account. Whether you transfer them into a personal checking account or a business checking account depends on how you plan to structure the acquisition:

- Personal Checking Account: If you are making a down payment with personal funds, transfer the money into your personal account. This is common when the acquisition is structured as a personal investment or when you are directly responsible for the down payment.

- Business Checking Account: If the funds are tied to your LLC or business, transfer them into the business's checking account. This helps keep your personal and business finances separate, which is essential for legal and tax purposes. It's also important to establish a clear paper trail for the down payment.

In either case, the goal is to create a clear, documented history that shows the funds are readily available and have been in your possession for the required seasoning period.

2. Let the Funds Sit for 60 to 90 Days

The seasoning period typically lasts between 60 and 90 days, depending on the lender's requirements. During this time, avoid transferring large sums of money in or out of the account to prevent raising any red flags with the lender. The more stable and consistent the account activity appears, the better.

- No Large Withdrawals: Lenders may view large withdrawals as a sign that your financial situation is unstable, which could affect their decision to approve the loan.

- No Additional Large Deposits: Avoid depositing large sums of money from other sources during this time, as it may raise questions about the origin of the funds. Lenders want to see that the money you're using for the down payment is not coming from loans or undisclosed financing, which could complicate the approval process.

3. Maintain Sufficient Funds

Ensure that the balance of the account stays at or above the amount needed for the down payment throughout the seasoning period. If your acquisition requires a $100,000 down payment, the account should consistently reflect at least $100,000 for the full seasoning period.

- Consider Keeping a Buffer: To avoid accidentally dipping below the required amount (due to fees or automatic payments), keep a buffer of extra cash in the account. For example, if you need $100,000 for the down payment, consider keeping $105,000 or more to ensure the balance never falls below the required threshold.

4. Document the Source of Funds

Lenders will typically request documentation to verify the origin of the seasoned funds. They want to ensure the money is not borrowed or the result of a last-minute transaction. To satisfy this requirement, you'll need to provide:

- Bank Statements: Provide 60-90 days of bank statements showing the money sitting in your account. The statements should clearly reflect that the funds have not been moved around excessively or recently deposited from questionable sources.

- Proof of 0% Interest Funding: If the down payment funds were obtained through a 0% interest credit line, you may need to explain the source. Some lenders may request documentation showing the terms of your business credit card or line of credit to ensure it is not a high-interest loan disguised as cash.

- Other Income Sources: If any portion of the down payment comes from your income or other investments, provide documentation (e.g., pay stubs, investment statements, or tax returns) to verify these sources.

5. Prepare for the Loan Application

Once the funds have been seasoned, you'll be ready to apply for the SBA 7(a) loan or other business loans. When applying for the loan, you'll need to demonstrate that the down payment funds are seasoned and ready to be used in the acquisition. This typically involves:

- Submitting Bank Statements: Provide bank statements for the past 60-90 days that clearly show the seasoned funds.

- Completing Financial Disclosure Forms: You'll likely need to complete financial disclosure forms that detail your assets, liabilities, and sources of income. Be prepared to list your accounts and provide information on how the down payment funds were obtained.

- Showing Proof of Collateral: Depending on the type of loan, you may need to offer collateral in addition to the down payment. In some cases, the business you're acquiring will serve as collateral, but you may also need to provide personal assets as collateral.

Alternative Options for Seasoning Funds

While most lenders require you to season funds for 60 to 90 days, there are a few alternative options that may help if you need to expedite the process or if the seasoning requirement is causing complications:

1. Gifted Funds: Some lenders allow for gifted funds to be used as part of the down payment, but they still need to be documented properly. If a family member or business partner is gifting you the down payment, the funds may need to be seasoned in the same way, or the lender may require a letter confirming the gift.

2. Collateralized Loan: In some cases, you can use a personal or business asset as collateral to reduce the down payment requirement or bypass the seasoning requirement altogether. For example, if you have equity in a property or another business, you may be able to use this as collateral for the loan.

3. Capital Injection from Partners or Investors: If you have partners or investors contributing to the down payment, you may need to show that their capital has also been seasoned. Make sure all contributors understand the seasoning requirements and are prepared to provide the necessary documentation.

4. Rapid Reserves: Some lenders may accept rapid reserves, which are funds deposited in a lump sum that hasn't been seasoned for the full period but are otherwise verifiable. This option is more likely to be offered by alternative lenders, and it usually comes with stricter terms or higher interest rates. It's less common in traditional SBA loans but can be useful in time-sensitive acquisitions.

Avoiding Pitfalls During the Seasoning Period

1. Avoid Over-Borrowing: Lenders may scrutinize whether the down payment is derived from loans, especially if it's not clear how the 0% interest funding will be repaid. Make sure you have a clear plan for paying off the credit lines and demonstrate that the funds you're seasoning are stable and reliable.

2. Don't Co-Mingle Funds: If possible, keep your down payment funds in a dedicated account to avoid mixing them with other personal or business funds. This helps create a clear paper trail and prevents confusion when you provide documentation to the lender.

3. Keep Records of Everything: Maintain detailed records of all transfers, deposits, and financial transactions during the seasoning period. If a lender questions the source of funds,

having thorough documentation will help clear up any doubts and speed up the loan approval process.

Navigating the SBA 7(a) Loan Process

Step 5: Navigating the SBA 7(a) Loan Process

Securing an SBA 7(a) loan is a key step in funding your business acquisition. The 7(a) loan program, backed by the U.S. Small Business Administration (SBA), is designed to help small businesses secure financing under favorable terms. With the SBA 7(a) loan, you can access funds for purchasing an existing business, refinancing debt, and even covering working capital needs. In this step, we'll walk through the entire process, from determining your eligibility to completing the loan application, and we'll explain how to use this funding for your business acquisition.

Why Choose the SBA 7(a) Loan for Business Acquisition?

1. Low Down Payment Requirements: SBA 7(a) loans typically require a down payment of 10% to 20%, which is lower than many conventional business loans. This makes it accessible for borrowers who may not have a large amount of liquid capital.

2. Long Repayment Terms: The loan offers extended repayment terms—up to 10 years for working capital or 25 years for real estate purchases—allowing for smaller, more manageable monthly payments.

3. Competitive Interest Rates: SBA 7(a) loans offer competitive interest rates, generally ranging from 6% to 9%, which can make it a more affordable option than many traditional loans.

4. Government Guarantee: The SBA guarantees a portion of the loan, reducing the risk for lenders. This makes them more willing to lend to businesses that may not qualify for conventional loans, especially in cases where the borrower lacks sufficient collateral or has a limited credit history.

Step-by-Step Guide to Securing an SBA 7(a) Loan

1. Eligibility Check

Before starting the SBA loan process, it's crucial to ensure both you and the business you want to acquire meet the basic eligibility criteria set by the SBA. Here are some of the key requirements:

- For the Borrower:
  - Personal Credit Score: A strong personal credit score is essential. While the minimum score varies, aim for a score of 680 or higher to improve your chances of approval.
  - Collateral: While not always required, having collateral to secure the loan can strengthen your application.
  - Debt-to-Income Ratio: Your debt-to-income (DTI) ratio should be manageable. The lower the DTI, the better your chances of loan approval.

- For the Business Being Acquired:
  - Business History: The business must be operating for at least three years. Newly established businesses are typically ineligible for SBA 7(a) loans.
  - Cash Flow: The business must have positive cash flow, as this will be used to repay the loan.
  - Gross Revenue: The SBA 7(a) loan is intended for small businesses, so the business should meet the SBA's size standards, which vary by industry. However, for this guide's parameters, gross revenue of $1,000,000 to $3,000,000 and cash flow between $125,000 and $1,000,000 are within typical SBA requirements.

2. Find an SBA-Approved Lender

The SBA 7(a) loan program doesn't provide the funds directly; instead, the SBA partners with approved lenders (usually banks or credit unions) who provide the loan with SBA backing. Finding the right lender is critical to your success. Look for a lender that has experience with business acquisitions and is familiar with the SBA process.

- Start with Your Bank: If you already have a banking relationship, it's worth checking with them to see if they offer SBA loans. Having an existing relationship can streamline the process.

- Use the SBA's Lender Match Tool: The SBA offers an online tool called Lender Match to help connect you with lenders who specialize in SBA-backed loans.

- Preferred SBA Lenders: Some lenders are designated as "preferred lenders," meaning they have more authority to approve SBA loans without needing direct SBA approval. These lenders tend to have faster turnaround times.

3. Prepare the Required Documentation

The SBA 7(a) loan application process is thorough, and you'll need to provide detailed financial and business documentation to prove your ability to repay the loan. Here's a breakdown of the key documents you'll need to gather:

- Personal Financial Information:
    - Personal Financial Statement: This outlines your assets, liabilities, income, and expenses. It helps the lender assess your financial strength.
    - Tax Returns: Typically, you'll need to provide your personal tax returns for the last 2-3 years to demonstrate income consistency.
    - Credit Report: The lender will pull your credit report to assess your creditworthiness.

- Business Financial Information (for the business you're acquiring):
    - Tax Returns: The business's tax returns for the last three years are typically required. These help the lender assess the business's financial stability.
    - Profit and Loss Statements: Also known as an income statement, this document shows the business's revenue, costs, and expenses over a period of time.

- Balance Sheet: A balance sheet provides a snapshot of the business's assets, liabilities, and equity, offering insight into its financial health.
- Cash Flow Projections: Projections for the next 1-3 years, showing expected revenue, expenses, and cash flow, which demonstrate how the business will generate enough profit to repay the loan.

- Business Plan: Even though the business you're acquiring is established, lenders want to see how you plan to run and grow the business. Your business plan should include:
  - Executive Summary: A brief overview of the business, the acquisition, and your qualifications.
  - Operations Plan: Outline how you plan to manage the business, including staffing and leadership.
  - Marketing Plan: Describe how you'll attract and retain customers post-acquisition.
  - Financial Plan: Include your cash flow projections, break-even analysis, and anticipated return on investment (ROI).

4. Submit Your Loan Application

Once you've gathered the necessary documentation and identified a lender, it's time to submit your loan application. The process may differ slightly depending on the lender, but generally, it includes the following steps:

- Complete the SBA 7(a) Loan Application (Form 1919): This form provides the lender with basic information about you, the business you're acquiring, and the loan terms you're requesting.

- Submit Financial Documents: Include all personal and business financial documents that the lender requires, as outlined above.

- Provide Your Business Plan: Be prepared to submit a detailed business plan that demonstrates your ability to run the acquired business successfully.

- Collateral Information: While the SBA doesn't require collateral for loans under $350,000, loans above this amount will typically require some form of collateral. This could include real estate, equipment, or other business assets.

5. Work with the Lender During Underwriting

Once you've submitted the application, the lender will begin the underwriting process. During this stage, the lender reviews your financial documents and evaluates the business you're acquiring to determine whether it meets their lending criteria. Here's what happens:

- Credit Review: The lender will check your credit score and history to assess your creditworthiness.

- Business Valuation: The lender may request a formal appraisal of the business you're acquiring to ensure the asking price is fair. This step is crucial because the loan amount will depend on the business's valuation.

- Cash Flow Analysis: The lender will analyze the business's cash flow to ensure it generates enough profit to cover loan repayments.

- Collateral Evaluation: If collateral is required, the lender will assess the value of the assets you've offered as security for the loan.

6. Approval and Loan Closing

If the lender approves your loan, the next step is closing. At this point, you'll finalize the loan agreement and officially take possession of the business. Here's what happens during the closing process:

- Review Loan Terms: Carefully review the loan terms, including the interest rate, repayment schedule, and any collateral requirements. Make sure you understand your obligations and ask questions if anything is unclear.

- Sign the Loan Agreement: Once you're satisfied with the terms, you'll sign the loan agreement. This legally binds you to the loan's terms and conditions.

- Funds Disbursement: The lender will disburse the loan funds, which can be used to pay for the business acquisition, working capital, or other approved expenses. The funds are usually disbursed directly to the seller or to an escrow account, depending on the terms of the acquisition.

7. Take Possession of the Business

After the loan has closed and the funds are disbursed, you will officially take possession of the business. The transition period is critical to ensuring a smooth handover and successful operation of the business. Here's how to manage this phase:

- Integrate with Existing Staff: Meet with key employees, managers, and stakeholders to communicate your vision and reassure them of job stability. Retaining key staff can help maintain continuity in the business's operations.

- Implement Your Business Plan: Begin executing the business plan you presented to the lender, focusing on immediate operational improvements and any planned changes to increase profitability.

- Manage Cash Flow: Use the cash flow projections you created as part of your business plan to monitor income and expenses. Pay close attention to your working capital needs, especially during the first few months of ownership.

Additional Considerations for SBA 7(a) Loans

1. **Personal Guarantee:** For most SBA 7(a) loans, you'll need to provide a personal guarantee. This means that if the business fails to repay the loan, you are personally responsible for making the payments. This is an important factor to consider, as it puts your personal assets, such as your home or savings, at risk if the business cannot meet its financial obligations.

2. **Loan Fees:** SBA 7(a) loans come with certain fees, including a guarantee fee, which is a percentage of the loan amount (typically around 3% for loans over $700,000). These fees can be rolled into the loan amount, but it's important to understand the total cost of borrowing.

3. **Debt Service Coverage Ratio (DSCR):** Lenders use this ratio to assess whether the business generates enough cash flow to cover the loan payments. The DSCR is calculated by dividing the business's net operating income by its total debt service (loan payments). A DSCR of 1.25 or higher is typically required, meaning the business should generate at least $1.25 in cash flow for every $1.00 in debt obligations.

4. **Prepayment Penalties:** While SBA loans generally don't have prepayment penalties for terms under 15 years, it's still important to check with your lender. If your business is performing well and you want to pay off the loan early, make sure there are no penalties for doing so.

5. **Ongoing Financial Reporting:** After you secure the loan, lenders will require regular financial reports to ensure the business is on track. Be prepared to provide quarterly or annual financial statements, including profit and loss statements, balance sheets, and cash flow reports.

Exit Strategy Planning After Securing an SBA 7(a) Loan

As part of your business acquisition strategy, it's essential to think ahead about your exit strategy, whether after 5 or 10 years. This can help you maximize your investment, plan for growth, and achieve financial freedom. Here are some potential exit strategies:

1. Selling the Business After 5 to 10 Years

After building the business over 5 to 10 years, one of the most common exit strategies is selling it. A successful business with strong cash flow and profitability can fetch a significant multiple of its annual earnings (usually 3-5x the annual cash flow, depending on the industry).

- Prepare for Sale: To maximize the sale price, you'll need to ensure that the business is financially healthy, has clean financial records, and operates smoothly without too much owner involvement. Engage a business broker or advisor to help find qualified buyers.

- Exit Timing: Consider selling the business when market conditions are favorable, and your financial performance is at its peak. Buyers are willing to pay more when the business shows consistent growth.

2. Franchising the Business

If the business model is replicable, you might consider franchising. Franchising allows you to expand the business and generate additional revenue through franchise fees and royalties without personally managing every new location.

- Franchise Development: You'll need to formalize the business's operational systems, develop training programs, and create franchise agreements. Franchisees will operate under your brand, while you provide support and oversight.

3. Holding for Passive Income

After 10 years, the business may become largely self-sustaining, requiring minimal day-to-day involvement from you. In this scenario, you can continue to hold the business for steady passive income while delegating management to a trusted team or hiring an experienced manager to oversee operations.

- Key Consideration: Holding the business long-term can provide consistent cash flow and equity growth, especially if the business is in a stable, low-risk industry.

4. IPO or Partial Sale

For businesses with significant growth potential, an initial public offering (IPO) or partial sale to investors may be an attractive exit strategy. This allows you to cash out part of your equity while retaining some control and benefiting from future growth.

- Partial Sale to Private Equity: In some cases, private equity firms may be interested in buying a portion of the business. This can provide you with liquidity while still allowing you to participate in the business's future success.

Here's a comprehensive list of 15 platforms and resources where individuals can find businesses for sale:

1. BizBuySell
   - Website: www.bizbuysell.com
   - Overview: One of the largest online business-for-sale marketplaces, featuring a wide range of businesses across various industries.

2. BizQuest
   - Website: www.bizquest.com

- Overview: Another major online business marketplace with thousands of business listings in various sectors, including franchises and small businesses.

3. BusinessBroker.net
   - Website: www.businessbroker.net
   - Overview: A business-for-sale platform that connects business buyers and sellers with a variety of listings, from small to medium-sized businesses.

4. LoopNet
   - Website: www.loopnet.com
   - Overview: Primarily known for commercial real estate, LoopNet also lists businesses for sale, particularly those with real estate components.

5. Flippa
   - Website: www.flippa.com
   - Overview: A marketplace for buying and selling online businesses, including websites, eCommerce stores, and apps.

6. MergerPlace
   - Website: www.mergerplace.com
   - Overview: A platform for buying and selling businesses, focusing on established companies and those involved in mergers and acquisitions.

7. BusinessesForSale.com
   - Website: www.businessesforsale.com
   - Overview: A global marketplace with over 60,000 business listings in various industries, including restaurants, retail, and service businesses.

8. Franchise Gator

- Website: www.franchisegator.com
  - Overview: Specializes in franchise opportunities, allowing users to browse franchises available for purchase.

9. Empire Flippers
   - Website: www.empireflippers.com
   - Overview: A marketplace for buying and selling profitable online businesses, including eCommerce stores, SaaS businesses, and content websites.

10. Exchange Marketplace (by Shopify)
    - Website: www.exchangemarketplace.com
    - Overview: Shopify's official marketplace for buying and selling eCommerce stores built on the Shopify platform.

11. Latona's
    - Website: www.latonas.com
    - Overview: Specializes in the sale of internet businesses, including SaaS, eCommerce, content-based websites, and domain names.

12. DealStream
    - Website: www.dealstream.com
    - Overview: A global business marketplace for buying and selling businesses, franchises, investment properties, and private equity opportunities.

13. Franchise Direct
    - Website: www.franchisedirect.com
    - Overview: A directory of franchise opportunities available for purchase, featuring franchises in various industries like food service, retail, and healthcare.

14. Transworld Business Advisors
   - Website: www.tworld.com
   - Overview: A global network of business brokers that helps buyers and sellers connect, specializing in small and medium-sized businesses.

15. Sunbelt Business Brokers
   - Website: www.sunbeltnetwork.com
   - Overview: One of the largest business brokerage networks in the U.S., with thousands of business-for-sale listings in various industries.

16. FE International
   - Website: www.feinternational.com
   - Overview: A mergers and acquisitions advisory firm specializing in the sale of SaaS, eCommerce, and content-based businesses.

17. Acquisitions Direct
   - Website: www.acquisitionsdirect.com
   - Overview: An online marketplace that focuses on established internet businesses for sale, including eCommerce, affiliate, and content websites.

18. BuyBusiness.com
   - Website: www.buybusiness.com
   - Overview: A user-friendly marketplace offering businesses for sale across different industries, with options for small to mid-sized enterprises.

19. IBBA (International Business Brokers Association)
   - Website: www.ibba.org

- Overview: Offers a directory of business brokers who list businesses for sale and can assist with the buying process.

  20. The Business Exchange
  - Website: www.thebizex.com
  - Overview: A business and franchise marketplace that lists businesses for sale in Canada and the U.S., focusing on small to medium-sized companies.

Conclusion

These 20 platforms and brokers provide an array of opportunities to find businesses for sale, from brick-and-mortar establishments to online and franchise options. Whether you're looking for a small local business or an international opportunity, these sites offer a comprehensive selection to fit a variety of interests and investment levels.

The formula used to evaluate a business's value based on a multiple of cash flow is designed to help potential buyers ensure that the business is profitable enough to service its debt and generate a return on investment. A common approach is to value the business at three times its annual cash flow (a 3x multiple). This valuation method is straightforward and is used in small to medium-sized business transactions, particularly for businesses with predictable cash flows.

 The Formula:
The basic formula for calculating a business's value using a 3x multiple of cash flow is:

Business Value = Cash Flow times 3

Where:
- Cash Flow is typically defined as the business's Seller's Discretionary Earnings (SDE) or Earnings Before Interest, Taxes, Depreciation, and Amortization (EBITDA).

- The 3x multiple is a commonly used rule of thumb for small businesses in industries where growth is stable, and debt servicing is realistic.

Key Terms Explained:

1. Cash Flow (SDE or EBITDA):
   - SDE (Seller's Discretionary Earnings): SDE represents the total financial benefit that the business generates for a single owner-operator. It includes the owner's salary, personal expenses paid by the business, and any other discretionary costs.
   - EBITDA (Earnings Before Interest, Taxes, Depreciation, and Amortization): This measure represents the business's profitability before accounting for non-operational expenses like interest, taxes, and depreciation. EBITDA is often used for larger businesses or those with a more complex financial structure.

2. 3x Multiple: The multiple reflects the industry, risk, and growth potential of the business. A 3x multiple is a standard assumption in small business transactions, though multiples can vary based on factors like market conditions, industry trends, and business size.

Ensuring Profitability and Debt Service

When evaluating a business at three times its cash flow, you need to ensure that the business generates enough cash flow to:
1. Pay the debt service (loan payments).
2. Cover operating expenses.
3. Provide a return on investment (ROI) for the buyer.

Let's break this down with an example.

Example:
Suppose you are considering buying a business with an annual cash flow (SDE) of $200,000. The business is being valued using a 3x multiple of cash flow.

Business Value = 200,000 times 3 = 600,000

This means the business is valued at $600,000. Let's say you finance the purchase through a loan with the following terms:
- Loan Amount: $540,000 (90% of the purchase price)
- Interest Rate: 6%
- Loan Term: 10 years

Using these terms, you can calculate the annual debt service (loan payments).

Calculating Annual Debt Service:
For a 10-year loan with a 6% interest rate, the formula for the annual debt payment (A) is:

$$A = \frac{P \times r \times (1+r)^n}{(1+r)^n - 1}$$

Where:

- A = Annual debt payment
- P = Loan principal (initial loan amount)
- r = Monthly interest rate (annual interest rate divided by 12)
- n = Total number of payments (number of years multiplied by 12 for monthly payments)

To use this formula:

1. Convert the annual interest rate to a monthly rate by dividing by 12 (for 6%, this would be 0.06/12 = 0.005).
2. Multiply the loan term in years by 12 to get the total number of payments (e.g., 10 years × 12 = 120 months).

3. Substitute the values into the formula to calculate the annual payment amount.

This formula will give the fixed annual payment required to repay the loan over 10 years at a 6% interest rate.

After performing the calculation, the annual debt service is approximately $72,000.

Ensuring Profitability:
To determine if the business can support the debt service and still be profitable, we subtract the annual debt payment from the cash flow:

Net Cash Flow After Debt Service} = 200,000 - 72,000 = 128,000

This $128,000 represents the amount left over after the debt payments, which should be sufficient to:
- Cover other operating expenses.
- Provide you with a reasonable salary and profit.

Ensuring Sustainability

To ensure that the business can comfortably pay off the loan, you would generally aim for the Debt Service Coverage Ratio (DSCR), which is calculated as:

$$DSCR = \frac{\text{Net Operating Income}}{\text{Total Debt Service}}$$

Where:

- **Net Operating Income** = Cash flow from operations or earnings before interest, taxes, depreciation, and amortization (EBITDA).
- **Total Debt Service** = The total annual debt payments, including both principal and interest.

A DSCR of **1.25 or higher** is typically required by lenders, meaning the business generates at least 25% more cash than is needed for debt payments. A higher DSCR indicates a stronger ability to meet debt obligations, making it a critical metric in assessing the financial health and risk of a business acquisition.

Summary:
- Business Valuation: The business is valued at 3x cash flow ($600,000 in this case), which is a standard multiple for small businesses.
- Debt Service: With an annual debt payment of $72,000 and cash flow of $200,000, the business generates enough cash flow to cover the debt service and still leave a healthy profit.
- Profitability: After debt payments, there is $128,000 left, which should be enough to cover operating costs and provide a return on investment.

Using the 3x multiple formula ensures that the business generates sufficient cash flow to pay down debt while remaining profitable and sustainable.

Here's a list of viable banking institutions that offer SBA 7(a) loans, with two options from each U.S. time zone:

Eastern Time Zone (ET)

1. Live Oak Bank (Wilmington, NC)
   - Overview: Live Oak Bank is one of the top SBA lenders in the country, consistently ranked as one of the largest SBA 7(a) lenders by volume. They specialize in various industries and are known for their streamlined application process and efficient customer service.
   - SBA 7(a) Loan Focus: Business acquisitions, franchise financing, real estate.

2. TD Bank (Cherry Hill, NJ)
   - Overview: TD Bank is a major SBA lender, offering competitive rates and personalized service. Their SBA 7(a) loans are ideal for small businesses looking to expand, purchase real estate, or acquire a new business.
   - SBA 7(a) Loan Focus: Business expansion, real estate, working capital.

Central Time Zone (CT)

1. Huntington National Bank (Columbus, OH)
   - Overview: Huntington Bank is one of the leading SBA 7(a) lenders in the Central time zone and across the U.S. They offer a wide range of SBA loans and are particularly well-regarded for their small business banking services.
   - SBA 7(a) Loan Focus: Business acquisitions, real estate, equipment financing.

2. BBVA USA (Houston, TX)
   - Overview: BBVA USA, now part of PNC Bank, is a top-tier SBA lender known for its personalized customer service and strong support for small businesses. They provide SBA 7(a) loans for a variety of needs, including business purchases and refinancing.
   - SBA 7(a) Loan Focus: Business acquisitions, real estate, working capital.

Mountain Time Zone (MT)

1. Zions Bank (Salt Lake City, UT)
   - Overview: Zions Bank has a strong reputation in the Mountain time zone for providing SBA 7(a) loans to small businesses. They offer tailored loan solutions and extensive resources for entrepreneurs.
   - SBA 7(a) Loan Focus: Business expansion, franchise financing, equipment purchases.

2. FirstBank (Lakewood, CO)
   - Overview: FirstBank is a large community bank with a strong SBA lending program. They offer competitive terms and are known for supporting businesses across various industries.
   - SBA 7(a) Loan Focus: Business acquisitions, working capital, commercial real estate.

Pacific Time Zone (PT)

1. Wells Fargo (San Francisco, CA)
   - Overview: Wells Fargo is one of the largest SBA lenders in the U.S. and has a strong presence in the Pacific time zone. They offer a variety of SBA loan products with competitive rates and a streamlined application process.
   - SBA 7(a) Loan Focus: Business acquisitions, equipment financing, working capital.

2. Umpqua Bank (Portland, OR)
   - Overview: Umpqua Bank is a regional bank known for its commitment to small business lending and personalized service. They provide flexible SBA 7(a) loan options for entrepreneurs and growing businesses.
   - SBA 7(a) Loan Focus: Business acquisitions, real estate, franchise financing.

Taking Possession and Transitioning

Step 6: Taking Possession and Transitioning

Once the SBA 7(a) loan has been approved and the acquisition funds are disbursed, you officially take possession of the business. This is a critical phase of the business acquisition process, where your leadership, strategic planning and relationship-building skills come into play. Transitioning smoothly ensures minimal disruption to operations, helps retain key employees, and sets the foundation for future growth. In this step, we'll cover how to manage the transition, integrate into the company's culture, optimize operations, and lay the groundwork for long-term success.

Why the Transition Period is Crucial

The first few months after acquiring a business are pivotal. This period involves:
- Understanding the Business: Although due diligence gives you an overview, operating the business yourself reveals the finer details of the day-to-day operations.
- Managing Key Relationships: From employees to customers and suppliers, maintaining and nurturing these relationships is vital to ensuring stability during the transition.
- Implementing Changes Thoughtfully: While you may have grand plans to improve efficiency, it's important to avoid making sweeping changes too quickly. A measured approach to change will help you build trust and avoid disrupting the company's core operations.

Step-by-Step Guide to a Smooth Transition

1. Take Stock of the Business's Current State

Before making any significant changes, spend time getting familiar with the business as it currently operates. This includes understanding the company's culture, operations, finances, and customer relationships. A thorough analysis will give you insights into areas that need improvement while highlighting what's already working well.

- Meet with the Previous Owner: If possible, spend time with the previous owner during the handover period. Their insights into how the business operates, key customers and potential challenges can be invaluable.
- Review Financials in Detail: Look beyond the surface numbers you examined during due diligence. Dig deeper into the company's accounts receivable, inventory management, expense trends, and cash flow. This will help you understand the business's true financial health and highlight any inefficiencies.
- Analyze Employee Roles: Get a clear understanding of each employee's role, responsibilities, and strengths. This will help you maintain continuity and determine if any changes are needed down the line.

2. Retain Key Staff and Build Trust

One of the most important aspects of a smooth transition is maintaining relationships with key staff members. Employees are often anxious about changes when new ownership takes over, so building trust and reassuring them of their value to the business is critical.

- Communicate Transparently: Hold meetings with the staff to introduce yourself, share your vision for the future, and address any concerns they may have. Emphasize continuity and your commitment to maintaining job security and improving the business.

- Identify Key Personnel: Pay special attention to key personnel, such as managers or long-serving employees, who hold institutional knowledge. These individuals can be instrumental in helping you understand the company's operations and ensuring a smooth transition.

- Offer Incentives for Retention: Consider offering incentives, such as bonuses or profit-sharing, to retain key employees during the transition period. Keeping talent in place reduces disruption and allows you to focus on growth rather than replacing critical staff.

3. Evaluate and Optimize Operations

Once you've familiarized yourself with the business's operations and stabilized relationships with employees, you can start looking for ways to improve efficiency. However, take a gradual approach—making too many changes too quickly can lead to confusion and resistance.

- Assess Workflow and Processes: Review the business's workflows, from production to customer service, to identify inefficiencies. Are there outdated systems or manual processes that could be automated? Are there bottlenecks in the supply chain that slow down production or service delivery?

- Implement Operational Improvements: Once you've identified areas for improvement, begin implementing changes gradually. For example:
    - Introduce new software to streamline inventory management.
    - Automate repetitive tasks, such as billing or data entry, to save time and reduce human error.
    - Redesign the layout of the workspace or streamline processes to improve efficiency and productivity.

- Negotiate with Vendors: Review contracts with suppliers and service providers. You may be able to renegotiate terms or find alternative vendors who can provide better pricing or more reliable service. This can have an immediate positive impact on the business's profitability.

4. Strengthen Customer Relationships

Maintaining strong relationships with the business's existing customers is essential for ensuring steady revenue during and after the transition. Early in your ownership, reach out to key customers to introduce yourself, reassure them of your commitment to service, and address any concerns.

- Communicate Your Vision: Send a personalized message to key customers explaining the acquisition and how you plan to maintain or improve the quality of service. Ensure customers that their needs will continue to be a priority.

- Gather Feedback: Use the transition as an opportunity to ask customers for feedback. What do they like about the business? What areas need improvement? This feedback will be invaluable as you shape your growth strategy.

- Implement a Customer Retention Plan: Put systems in place to reward customer loyalty, such as loyalty programs, discounts, or enhanced customer service efforts. This can help reinforce customer relationships and ensure they remain engaged with the business.

5. Manage Financials and Cash Flow

Managing cash flow is one of the most important aspects of running a business, especially in the early stages of ownership. Keep a close eye on income, expenses, and working capital needs during the transition period.

- Monitor Accounts Receivable: Stay on top of invoices and collections. Ensure that outstanding payments are being collected in a timely manner to maintain cash flow.

- Keep Operating Expenses in Check: Review the business's operating expenses and look for opportunities to reduce costs without compromising quality. This may include renegotiating leases, reviewing utility costs, or identifying areas where you can streamline operations.

- Maintain a Cash Flow Buffer: It's always a good idea to have a buffer of cash reserves to handle any unexpected expenses or slowdowns in revenue. If the business is seasonal, prepare for potential fluctuations in income during off-peak times.

6. Implement Your Business Plan Gradually

While it's important to have a vision and strategy for growth, implementing changes too quickly can backfire. Take a phased approach to executing your business plan, focusing first on the low-hanging fruit—areas where small improvements can have a significant impact on profitability.

- Set Short-Term Goals: Identify a few key areas for improvement in the first 90 days of ownership, such as improving customer service, optimizing inventory, or streamlining operations.

- Measure Performance: Track key performance indicators (KPIs) to measure the impact of your changes. This could include metrics like profit margins, customer satisfaction scores, employee productivity, or inventory turnover.

- Adjust the Plan as Needed: Be flexible. If certain strategies aren't working as expected, don't hesitate to adjust your approach. The early months of ownership will teach you a lot about the business and its market, so use this information to refine your long-term growth strategy.

7. Consider an Exit Strategy Early

Even as you're taking control of the business, it's never too early to start thinking about your exit strategy. Whether you plan to sell the business in 5 or 10 years or hold it for passive income, having a long-term vision will guide your decisions and ensure that you're building the business's value.

- Increase Business Valuation: Focus on growth strategies that will enhance the business's profitability, making it more attractive to potential buyers or investors in the future.

- Develop Succession Plans: If you plan to exit the business eventually, start thinking about succession early. Whether it's selling to a third party or passing the business on to family or employees, having a plan in place will ensure a smoother transition when the time comes.

Key Considerations During the Transition

1. Cultural Sensitivity: If the business has a strong company culture, it's important to respect and preserve it during the transition. Employees and customers may be resistant to sudden changes, so take the time to understand the existing culture before making any major shifts.

2. Legal Compliance: Make sure that all legal and regulatory requirements are met as you take ownership of the business. This includes updating licenses, permits, and registrations with the appropriate government agencies.

3. Technology Integration: If the business's technology is outdated or inefficient, consider gradually implementing new systems to improve efficiency. However, be mindful of the disruption this can cause, and ensure that proper training is provided to employees.

4. Customer and Vendor Contracts: Review any long-term contracts the business has with customers or vendors. Make sure they align with your goals for the business and consider renegotiating terms if needed.

Exit Strategy Options After 5 and 10 Years

Step 7: Exit Strategy Options After 5 and 10 Years

Once you've successfully acquired and operated your business, it's essential to plan for the future—particularly your exit strategy. Having a well-defined exit plan helps you maximize the value of the business and achieve your long-term financial goals, whether that's selling the business, franchising it, or holding it for passive income. In this step, we'll explore several exit strategies that you can consider after 5 and 10 years of ownership, ensuring that your efforts in building the business lead to profitable outcomes.

Why Having an Exit Strategy is Important

1. Maximizing Value: The way you exit the business will significantly impact your financial returns. By planning early, you can implement strategies to increase the business's valuation and ensure a smooth transition when it's time to exit.

2. Flexibility: A well-thought-out exit strategy provides flexibility. Whether market conditions, personal goals, or industry changes influence your decision, having an exit plan allows you to adapt without being forced into a rushed or unplanned sale.

3. Succession Planning: Whether you plan to sell the business, transition to a family member, or sell part of it to investors, a clear exit strategy ensures that the process is smooth and leaves the business in capable hands.

Step-by-Step Guide to Exit Strategy Options

1. Sell the Business After 5 to 10 Years

One of the most common exit strategies is selling the business, either partially or entirely. Selling after 5 to 10 years allows you to capitalize on the value you've built in the business and achieve a profitable return on your investment. Here's how to approach selling your business strategically:

1.1. Prepare the Business for Sale

To maximize the sale price, it's essential to ensure that the business is in top financial and operational shape. Buyers are looking for profitable, well-run businesses with clear potential for growth. Here's how to prepare:

- Clean Financial Records: Ensure that your financial records are clear, transparent, and well-documented. This includes up-to-date profit and loss statements, balance sheets, tax returns, and cash flow reports. Buyers will closely scrutinize these documents, so make sure they reflect the health of the business.

- Optimize Operations: Streamline your business's operations to make it as efficient and profitable as possible. This could include reducing unnecessary expenses, automating processes, or optimizing supply chains. A more efficient business is more attractive to potential buyers.

- Develop Standard Operating Procedures (SOPs): Buyers want to see that the business can run smoothly without you. Document your business processes in detailed SOPs so that the new owner can easily take over. This increases the perceived value of the business because it shows it can operate independently of its current owner.

- Diversify Revenue Streams: If possible, diversify your sources of revenue to reduce dependence on a single product, service, or customer. This will make the business more resilient and valuable in the eyes of buyers.

1.2. Valuation and Pricing

Valuing a business is both an art and a science. The valuation typically depends on factors such as profitability, market conditions, industry trends, and growth potential. Here's how to approach pricing:

- Multiple of Earnings (EBITDA): One common method for valuing a business is using a multiple of its EBITDA (Earnings Before Interest, Taxes, Depreciation, and Amortization). For small businesses, the typical multiple ranges from 3x to 5x EBITDA, depending on the industry. For example, if your business generates $300,000 in EBITDA annually, the selling price could be between $900,000 and $1,500,000.

- Market Comparisons: Another method is to compare your business to similar businesses that have been sold recently. Industry brokers can help you find comparable sales to determine a reasonable asking price.

- Future Growth Potential: Buyers are willing to pay more for businesses with strong future growth potential. Highlight any opportunities for expansion, new markets, or product lines to justify a higher price.

1.3. Finding Buyers

Once your business is prepared for sale, you'll need to find qualified buyers. You can take several approaches:

- Business Brokers: A business broker specializes in helping business owners sell their companies. They can help you value the business, find qualified buyers, and negotiate the sale.

- Private Equity Firms: If your business is large enough or has significant growth potential, private equity firms may be interested in acquiring it. These firms typically look for businesses that can be scaled or improved for a profitable exit down the road.

- Strategic Buyers: Strategic buyers are companies in your industry looking to expand their operations or acquire new capabilities. They may be willing to pay a premium for your business if it aligns with their strategic goals.

1.4. Negotiating the Sale

When negotiating the sale, focus on the terms that are most important to you, such as:

- Price: While the final selling price is critical, consider other factors such as the payment structure. Will you receive the full amount upfront, or will it be paid in installments?

- Seller Financing: In some cases, you may offer seller financing, where the buyer pays a portion of the purchase price over time. This can be an attractive option for buyers who need flexible payment terms, and it may allow you to negotiate a higher overall price.

- Transition Period: Buyers may ask for your help during a transition period after the sale. Be clear about how long you're willing to stay involved and what your role will be.

2. Franchise the Business

If your business model is scalable, you may want to consider franchising as a long-term exit strategy. Franchising allows you to replicate your business in multiple locations while earning revenue through franchise fees and royalties.

2.1. Develop a Franchise System

Franchising requires that you create a replicable system that franchisees can follow to operate their businesses successfully. Here's how to develop a franchise system:

- Standardize Operations: Create detailed operating manuals, training programs, and marketing guidelines that franchisees can follow. The more standardized your processes, the easier it will be to replicate the business.

- Legal Requirements: Franchising requires legal documentation, including a Franchise Disclosure Document (FDD) that outlines the terms and conditions of the franchise agreement. You'll need to work with a franchise attorney to develop this document and ensure you comply with federal and state regulations.

- Build a Support Structure: Successful franchises provide ongoing support to franchisees. This includes marketing support, training, and operational assistance. Make sure you have the resources in place to provide this support as your franchise network grows.

2.2. Recruit Franchisees

To grow your franchise, you'll need to recruit qualified franchisees. Here's how to find the right candidates:

- Target Market: Identify potential franchisees who are passionate about your industry and have the necessary financial resources to invest in the franchise.

- Marketing Your Franchise: Use online franchise directories, trade shows, and industry publications to market your franchise opportunity to potential investors.

3. Hold the Business for Passive Income

If the business becomes self-sustaining and generates consistent cash flow, you may decide to hold it for passive income rather than selling it. This strategy allows you to benefit from the business's profitability while minimizing your involvement.

3.1. Delegate Day-to-Day Operations

To make the business run independently of you, hire a general manager or executive team to oversee daily operations. This allows you to step back and focus on high-level strategic decisions without being involved in the day-to-day management of the business.

3.2. Maintain Cash Flow

Holding the business requires careful attention to cash flow management. Make sure you have systems in place to monitor revenue, expenses, and profits, and stay involved enough to ensure the business continues to grow and maintain its profitability.

4. IPO or Partial Sale

For businesses with significant growth potential, taking the company public through an Initial Public Offering (IPO) or selling part of the business to investors can be a lucrative exit strategy.

4.1. Prepare for IPO

Taking your business public involves a rigorous process of financial auditing, regulatory compliance, and market preparation. You'll need to work with investment bankers, accountants, and legal advisors to ensure the business is ready to go public.

4.2. Partial Sale to Investors

Selling a portion of the business to private investors or private equity firms can provide liquidity while still allowing you to retain some control. This strategy works well if you want to cash out part of your equity while continuing to participate in the business's future growth.

Glossary of Business Acquisition Terms

Glossary of Business Acquisition Terms

This glossary covers key terms and concepts used in the realm of business acquisition, with definitions based on the steps outlined in the acquisition process. These terms will help clarify the language commonly used when buying, selling, and financing businesses.

Acquisition
The process of buying an existing business or company. In a business acquisition, the buyer takes over the operations, assets, and often liabilities of the target business.

Amortization
The gradual repayment of a loan over time through scheduled payments. In business acquisitions, loan payments often include both principal and interest, which are amortized over the loan's term.

Annual Debt Service
The total yearly payment required to repay the principal and interest on a loan. This is a critical figure when determining whether a business generates enough cash flow to cover its loan obligations.

Business Valuation
The process of determining the value or worth of a business. A common valuation method is applying a multiple (such as 3x) to the business's cash flow or earnings.

Cash Flow
The net amount of cash generated by a business after all expenses have been paid. Cash flow can be used to assess the business's profitability and ability to cover debt obligations.

Common measures include Seller's Discretionary Earnings (SDE) and Earnings Before Interest, Taxes, Depreciation, and Amortization (EBITDA).

Collateral
Assets that a borrower offers to a lender as security for a loan. If the borrower defaults, the lender can seize the collateral to recoup losses. In business acquisition loans, collateral may include business assets or personal property.

Debt Service Coverage Ratio (DSCR)
A financial ratio used to measure a business's ability to cover its debt payments with its operating income.

A DSCR of 1.25 or higher is generally required by lenders, meaning the business generates 25% more cash than is needed to cover loan payments.

Due Diligence
The investigative process is conducted by a buyer before acquiring a business. Due diligence includes reviewing financial records, legal contracts, operations, employee information, and other key areas to assess the health and value of the business.

Earnings Before Interest, Taxes, Depreciation, and Amortization (EBITDA)
A measure of a company's operating performance, often used to evaluate its profitability without the impact of financial decisions (interest and taxes) or non-cash expenses (depreciation and amortization). It is commonly used in business valuations.

Franchise
A business model is where a company (franchisor) grants a license to an individual (franchisee) to operate a business using its brand, products, and systems. In a business acquisition context, franchises may be purchased as turnkey operations.

Interest Rate
The percentage charged by a lender for borrowing money is usually expressed as an annual percentage rate (APR). In business acquisitions, lower interest rates can reduce the overall cost of the loan.

Loan-to-Value Ratio (LTV)
A financial term used by lenders to compare the amount of a loan to the value of the asset being purchased. For business acquisitions, the LTV ratio helps determine how much of the business's purchase price can be financed by a loan.

Multiple (Valuation Multiple)
A financial metric used to estimate the value of a business, often expressed as a multiple of cash flow or EBITDA. A 3x multiple, for example, means the business is valued at three times its annual cash flow.

Operating Agreement
A legal document used in Limited Liability Companies (LLCs) that outlines the ownership structure, roles, responsibilities, and operating procedures of the business. It is essential for businesses with multiple owners.

Personal Guarantee
A legal commitment made by an individual (usually the business owner) to repay a loan if the business cannot meet its obligations. In SBA loans and other financing, personal guarantees are often required.

Seller's Discretionary Earnings (SDE)
A measure of a business's cash flow that represents the total financial benefit available to a single owner. SDE includes the owner's salary, benefits, and discretionary expenses. It is commonly used in valuing small businesses.

Seasoning

The process of leaving funds in a bank account for a specified period (usually 60 to 90 days) to prove they are stable and ready for use, such as for a down payment in a business acquisition. Seasoned funds increase lender confidence.

Standard Operating Procedures (SOPs)
Documented guidelines and instructions for performing routine tasks in a business. SOPs are critical during a business acquisition to ensure continuity and efficiency as the new owner takes control.

SBA 7(a) Loan
A loan program offered by the U.S. Small Business Administration (SBA) that provides funding for small business acquisitions, expansions, and working capital. The SBA guarantees a portion of the loan, reducing the lender's risk.

Transition Period
The time immediately following a business acquisition when the new owner takes over and begins operating the business. During this period, the buyer integrates with the existing team, stabilizes operations, and implements changes.

Working Capital
The capital a business uses for its day-to-day operations, is calculated as current assets minus current liabilities. Adequate working capital ensures the business can cover its operational expenses and stay solvent.

Zero Percent Interest Funding
A financing strategy where borrowers secure credit or loans with a 0% interest rate for an introductory period, typically 12 months. This funding can be used for business acquisitions or working capital without incurring immediate interest costs.

---

www.ingramcontent.com/pod-product-compliance
Lightning Source LLC
Chambersburg PA
CBHW070347230526
45471CB00006B/2461